The Best 45 Freezer Meals

Your Money-Saving, Quick and Easy,
Convenient, Make Ahead Recipes

Disclaimer

Effort has been made to ensure that the information in this book is accurate and complete. However, the author and the publisher do not warrant the accuracy of the information, text and graphics contained within the book due to the rapidly changing nature of science, research, known and unknown facts. The author and the publisher do not hold any responsibility for errors, omissions or contrary interpretation of the subject matter herein. This book is presented solely for motivational and informational purposes only.

All Rights Reserved.

No part of this publication or the information in it may be quoted from or reproduced in any form by means such as printing, scanning, photocopying or otherwise without prior written permission of the copyright holder.

Before You Start

Hello!

First of all I'm very proud of combining the Best-Seller "Easy Freezer Meals: Your Money-Saving, Easy and Convenient Make Ahead Recipes" and the huge success "Freezer Meals for an Easy Life: Your Money-Saving, Quick and Convenient Make Ahead Recipes" into a complete collection. It's a bargain for sure!

With 45 delicious recipes you will never run out of ideas for your easy freezer meals!

If this is the first time you read any of these volumes just keep reading!

However if you already read any of these books feel free to go straight to the awesome recipes just for you!

Enjoy!

Other Books by Morgan White

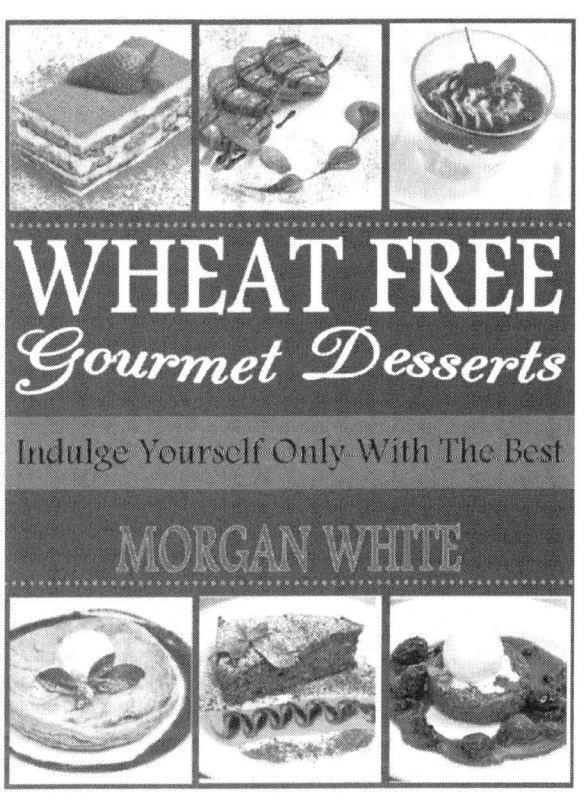

Table of Contents

Before You Start 3
Freezing Meals...For What? 9
Tips You Should Know 11
About Bulk Buying 13
Conversions 15
Chicken Freezer Meals 16
    Chicken Enchiladas 17
    Chicken Nuggets 19
    Garlic-thyme Chicken 21
    Teriyaki Chicken 23
    Creamy Chicken 25
    Chicken Burgers 27
    Chicken Black Bean Chili 29
    Chicken Pie 31
    Chicken Bites with Pineapple 34
    Chicken Croquettes 38
    Chicken Casserole 41
Seafood Freezer Meals 43
    Pink Salmon Cakes 44
    Clam Chowder 46

Frozen Cod 49

Frozen Stuffed Clams 51

Frozen Tilapia with Bell Peppers 54

Crab Soup 57

Freezer Shrimps with Cabbage 59

Horseradish Tilapia Cakes 63

Simple Salmon Loaf 66

Orange Salmon with Veggies 68

Creole Shrimps with Couscous 70

Spicy Red Snapper with Cooked Rice 73

Seafood Chowder 75

Pork Freezer Meals 78

Pork and Plums 79

Almond Meal Breaded Pork Chops 81

Apple Pork Chops 84

Pork Meatballs 86

Green Peppers Stuffed with Pork 88

Pork Casserole 91

Pork Tenderloin with Beer 93

Mustard Pork Chops with Applesauce 95

Spicy Pork Soup 98

Pork Pies 101

Pork Empanadas 104

Vegetarian Freezer Meals 108

Black Bean Burgers 109
Vegetarian Chili 111
Vegetarian Calzones 114
Vegetable Soup 116
Chickpea Pot Pie 119
Quinoa Cakes 121
Rice Herbs and Cheese Balls 123
Eggplant Lasagna.. 126
Stuffed Peppers 129
Vegetable Stew.. 132

Conclusion...135
Did you like this book? 136
Highly Recommended...............................137
Other Books by Morgan White 138

Freezing Meals…For What?

Freezing meals has a lot of advantages.

Just to start it's incredible how much money you can save buying foods in bulk!

Imagine you receive unexpected visits. Now what? Easy: just reheat one of your already extra tasty frozen meals!

If you're anything like me you probably hate cooking every single night. Now you don't have to: with some planning in advance you will only have to cook 2-3 nights a week. It really is a stress reliever!

The thing I enjoy the most about freezing meals is the better lifestyle it gives me. I'm not just talking about the money saving, although that's important for sure. I'm talking about getting home from work, after a stressful day, and be able to lie down on my favorite couch and know that I won't have to prepare any meal for that day.

If you're a lady just imagine: getting home, doing your nails and watching your favorite TV show while enjoying a glass of wine.

Or if you're a guy, like me, picture this: grabbing a cold one, heading for the living room and just chill while watching your favorite sport. Hmm, sounds good to me!

Tips You Should Know

Most ingredients, when frozen, can last from 1-2 months up to 4 months. Some even go as far as 12 months. I'm not telling you this for testing those limits but to show you the considerable window of opportunity you have to prepare those tasty meals.

Usually whole cuts of uncooked meat or large pieces of whole cuts will last more in the freezer than small pieces.

Air around the food isn't helpful at all, so you should seal the ingredients the best you can.

Foods that freeze well: seafood, fish, meat, bread, soups, stews, stock, most vegetables, cheese, ham, bacon, ginger, fresh chili, horseradish, pastry, cooked rice, berries, bananas and herbs.

Foods that don't freeze well: tomato, celery, spinach, lettuce, cucumber, lettuce, most dairy products (except cheese), raw potatoes, mayonnaise and cream sauces, whole eggs and jam.

Although freezing food slows down harmful bacteria, it doesn't kill it, so avoid refreezing raw food or any food for that matter.

In the beginning I would forget which frozen meal was in each container. <u>Not anymore:</u> get yourself a sharpie and painters tape and mark all containers with the cooking instructions and the date you made it.

You cooked something and it's still hot or, at least, warm. What should you do? Let it cool completely before freezing it.

Before eating thaw the ingredients, or the meals, in the refrigerator for 12-24 hours. Make sure you put it on a plate that can contain leaks.

About Bulk Buying

Once you get the hang of freezing meals (and feel the improvement on the quality of your life) you will probably think about getting an extra freezer. You can find some good ones in the $100-$200 range of price.

Once you start looking for bulk buying options you will probably come to the same conclusions than me:

- Products in season are cheaper and tastier.

- Meats on large packages are cheaper.

- Some warehouse clubs or grocery stores lower the price of some categories of ingredients always at the same period of time (example: week to week, or every second week). Learn about it and buy those particular ingredients in big quantities during those days.

- You will discover that some products are cheaper online, so give it a try.

My favorite options for storing things in the freezer are plastic deli containers, zip-lock bags and aluminum foil pans. You can use them multiple times and, because they are very affordable you won't feel bad when you need to get rid of them.

Conversions

1 cup = 237 ml (milliliters)

1 teaspoon = 5 ml

1 tablespoon = 15 ml = 3 teaspoons

1 Oz (liquids) = 30 ml

8 Oz (liquids) = 1 cup

1 Oz = 28 grams

1 inch = 2.54 cm (centimeters)

1lb. = 454 gr. (grams)

1 quart = 946 ml

4 cups = 1 quart

1 pint = 550 ml

Chicken Freezer Meals

Chicken Enchiladas

Serving: 6

Preparation: 30 min.

Cooking: 15 min.

Reheat: 25 min.

Ingredients:

- 1 ½ pounds chicken breasts, cooked and shredded
- 17 oz. enchilada sauce, preserve 1 ½ cups
- 5 oz. chopped green chilies
- 17 oz. black beans, rinsed
- 12 tortillas
- 6 oz. shredded cheese – by your choice
- 2 teaspoons smoked paprika

Preparation method:

1. Combine shredded chicken meat, enchilada sauce green chilies, black beans and smoked paprika in a large greased skillet.
2. Simmer for 15 minutes and set aside to cool.
3. Place a spoonful of prepared mixture into tortilla wraps, and wrap firmly.
4. Arrange in greased oven-proof baking dish and pour over remaining sauce; top with cheese.

Freezing instructions:

1. Cover baking dish with aluminum foil and keep in the freezer until want to use.

Reheating instructions:

1. Thaw in refrigerator overnight. Remove from the refrigerator 30 minutes before baking.
2. Bake in preheated oven at 180C/350F for 20 minutes, covered.
3. Uncover and bake for 5 minutes more or until cheese is melted.

Chicken Nuggets

Serving: 6

Preparation time: 30 min.

Reheat time: 15 min.

Ingredients:

- 2 lb. chicken breasts, boneless
- 4 cups corn flakes
- 1 teaspoon garlic powder
- ½ cup flour
- 3 eggs, beaten
- Freshly ground salt and pepper
- ½ cup Parmesan cheese

Preparation method:

1. Cut chicken breasts in nugget size pieces.
2. Place corn flakes in firm plastic bag and crush using rolling pin.

3. Transfer to the large bowl and add garlic powder, salt, pepper and Parmesan cheese.
4. Beat eggs in another bowl and place flour in shallow dish.
5. To bread chicken meat, place in the flour, then the eggs and finally the cornflakes mixture.

Freezing method:

1. Place in wide bowl or in zip-lock bags and keep in freezer up to two weeks.

Reheating method:

1. Thaw in refrigerator overnight and remove 30 minutes before baking.
2. Preheat oven to 200C/400F and line baking tray with parchment paper.
3. Spread chicken nuggets onto baking tray and bake for 15 minutes or until golden.
4. Serve immediately.

Garlic-thyme Chicken

Serving: 6

Preparation time: 20 min.

Reheat and cooking time: 20 min.

Ingredients:

- 3 lb. chicken breasts, boneless
- 2 cups cooking cream
- 1 cup mayonnaise
- 3 tablespoons garlic, minced
- 2 springs thyme, chopped
- Freshly ground salt
- 1 teaspoon cayenne pepper

Preparation method:

1. Slice chicken breasts in small fillets.
2. Combine rest or ingredients in a large bowl and add chicken slices.

Freezing method:

1. Stir well to coat chicken and transfer all to the zip-lock bag.
2. Place in the freezer and keep until ready to use.

Reheating and cooking method:

1. Place in the refrigerator overnight or until thawed.
2. Preheat grill pan and coat with some oil.
3. Add chicken, with sauce and cook for 20 minutes or until chicken is tender and sauce reduced.
4. Serve immediately.

Teriyaki Chicken

Serving: 6

Preparation time: 10 min.

Reheating and cooking time: 15 min.

Ingredients:

- 3 large chicken breast fillets, sliced
- 1 cup teriyaki sauce
- 1 cup water
- 3 teaspoons grated ginger
- 3 tablespoons honey
- 4 garlic cloves

Preparation method:

1. Place all ingredients in a large zip-lock bag.
2. Once the bag is firmly closed, shake it well, so all ingredients are combined.

Freezing method:

1. Place prepared chicken in the freezer and keep until ready to use.

Reheating and cooking method:

1. Soak the zip-lock bag in large bowl of hot water, for 2-3 minutes.
2. Gently remove the chicken and place in the oiled pan. Cover with lid.
3. Cook for 5 minutes on medium-high, or until cooked through.
4. Add teriyaki sauce and boil it, flipping the chicken until coated evenly.
5. The chicken is done when the most of sauce has vaporized, for 10 minutes.
6. Serve while still hot with fresh lime wedges.

Creamy Chicken

Serving: 6

Preparation method: 10 min.

Reheating and cooking time: 17 min.

Ingredients:

- 10 oz. chicken breasts, boneless
- 8 oz. soft creamy cheese
- 10 oz. can of cream chicken soup
- 1 teaspoon dried basil
- 1 teaspoon dried oregano
- ½ teaspoon dried mint

Preparation method:

1. Combine herbs, creamy cheese and cream chicken soup in a large bowl.

2. Stir well and place in the zip-lock bag. Add chicken slices and push the mixture so chicken is coated.

Freezing method:

1. Place the zip-lock bag in the freezer and keep until ready to use.

Reheating and cooking time:

1. Soak zip-lock bag in the warm water for 2 minutes.
2. Heat large skillet over medium-high heat and add chicken.
3. Cook for 15 minutes until chicken is tender.
4. Serve immediately.

Chicken Burgers

Serving: 6

Preparation time: 10 min.

Cooking time: 10 min.

Ingredients:

- 2 lb. ground chicken meat
- 1 teaspoon minced garlic
- 1 teaspoon dried basil
- 2 tablespoons lemon juice
- Freshly ground salt and pepper
- ½ cup fresh parsley, chopped
- 1 cup breadcrumbs
- 2 tablespoons olive oil
- 1 teaspoon ground cumin

Preparation method:

1. In a large bowl combine minced meat, garlic, parsley, basil, lemon juice, salt and pepper.
2. Form patties and set aside.

Freezing method:

1. Place the patties into container, lined with parchment paper.
2. Freeze and keep until ready to use.

Cooking method:

1. Defrost in the microwave or set in refrigerator overnight, until thawed.
2. Coat in breadcrumbs and heat olive oil in large skillet.
3. Cook patties over medium-high heat, until browned both sides, for 10 minutes.
4. Serve immediately.

Chicken Black Bean Chili

Serving: 6

Preparation time: 5 min.

Cooking time: 30 min.

Ingredients:

- 4 chicken breasts, cooked and shredded
- 40 oz. tomato sauce
- 30 oz. black beans, drained and rinsed
- 2 diced shallots
- 2 teaspoons garlic powder
- 4 teaspoons chili powder
- 2 teaspoons cumin
- 1 teaspoon red pepper flakes

Preparation method:

1. Combine all ingredients in a bowl and toss to coat chicken well.

Freezing method:

1. Place ingredients in a zip-lock bag and shake once again to coat the chicken.
2. Set in the freezer and keep until ready to use.

Cooking method:

1. Set the chicken in the refrigerator overnight to thaw.
2. Place all ingredients in the large pot or sauce pan and cook for 30 minutes.
3. Serve while still hot.

Chicken Pie

Serves: 6

Preparation time: 10 min.

Cooking time: 1 hour

Ingredients:

- 2 chicken breasts, cooked and shredded
- 1 cup broccoli florets
- 1 cup chopped carrots
- ½ cup corn
- 1 teaspoon onion powder
- 1 teaspoon garlic powder
- 1 teaspoon salt
- Fresh ground pepper – to taste
- 1 package pie crust – by your choice

Preparation method:

1. Place all ingredients in a bowl and toss to combine well.

2. Place in zip-lock bag and set in freezer.

Freezing method:

1. Lay the zip-lock bag to freezer, in flat position.
2. Freeze and keep until ready to use.

Cooking method:

1. Set the prepared mixture into refrigerator overnight to thaw.
2. Preheat oven to 180C/350F and grease pie pan with some oil. Roll out the two pie crust between 2 pieces parchment paper and place one on the bottom.
3. Place thawed ingredients in the prepared pie crust and cover with other crust. Pinch firmly to seal the edges and place in the preheated oven.
4. Bake for 1 hour and slice when cooled slightly.

NOTE: You can make the pie completely and freeze it that way, and after just bake at 180C/350F again for 1 hour.

Chicken Bites with Pineapple

Serves: 6

Preparation time: 15 min.

Cooking time: 8 min.

Reheating time: 20 min.

Ingredients:

- 1 lb. chicken, cut into bite sizes
- 1 cup all-purpose flour
- 3 tablespoons cornstarch
- 3 eggs
- Large pinch of salt
- Some vegetable oil – to fry

For the sauce:

- 14 oz. pineapple, diced, with juice
- ½ onion, finely chopped
- ½ cup water

- ½ green pepper, chopped
- ½ teaspoon salt
- 3 tablespoons apple cider vinegar
- 2 tablespoons cornstarch
- 2 tablespoons sugar

Preparation method:

1. Preheat oil in the Dutch oven on medium heat.
2. In a large bowl combine salt, flour and cornstarch.
3. Make a well in the center and crack in the eggs and add water.
4. Whisk well until you have smooth mixture and add sliced chicken; stir to coat well.
5. Using a fork drop chicken bites in the heated oil and cook for 3 minutes.
6. Set on paper towel to cool and drain.

Preparing the sauce:

1. Heat some oil in the sauce pan and cook onion, until starting to softened.

2. Add canned pineapple, sugar, vinegar and salt. Bring to a boil.
3. Combine the cornstarch and water in a separate bowl or cup until dissolved. Add to pineapple mixture along with green pepper. Simmer 2 minutes until thick.

Freezing method:

1. Place chicken bites in one zip-lock bag and sauce in other.
2. Place in the freezer, flat position and keep until ready to use.

Reheating method:

1. Soak zip-lock bag in bowl of hot water, for 6-8 minutes.
2. Preheat oven to 180C/350F and line baking tray with parchment paper.
3. Arrange chicken bites onto baking sheet and bake for 15-20 minutes or until crisp.
4. Sauce: set the sauce in the freezer overnight to thaw.

5. Place the sauce in sauce pan and heat over medium heat for 10 minutes.
6. Serve over chicken while still hot.

Chicken Croquettes

Serves: 6

Preparation time: 50 min.

Cooking time: 3 minutes

Ingredients:

- 2 ½ lb. chicken meat, preferably drumsticks
- 3 garlic cloves
- 6 tablespoons butter
- 2 eggs
- 1 cup breadcrumbs
- Fresh ground salt and pepper
- 1 onion, chopped
- ¾ cup flour
- ½ cup vegetable oil
- 1 large sweet potato, or 2 small
- 1/3 cup chicken stock

Preparation method:

1. Preheat oven to 220C/425F and line baking tray with aluminum foil.
2. Arrange chicken drumsticks onto baking tray and rub all over with two tablespoons butter.
3. Season with salt and pepper, add whole garlic cloves and wrap with the foil.
4. Bake for 45 minutes and set on wire rack to cool. Discard the skin and bones, and shred chicken meat finely.
5. Meanwhile stab the potato several times and place in the microwave; cook for 8-10 minutes. Peel the potato and place in the bowl; add reserved baked garlic and mash until you have fine puree.
6. In small sauce pan melt the remaining butter, over medium heat and add onion. Cook until softened, for 6-8 minutes.
7. Stir in ¼ cup flour and cook, stirring constantly, for 3 minutes. Gradually add the chicken stock and cook for 3 minutes more, stirring occasionally.
8. Combine prepared paste with the mashed potato and stir in shredded chicken; season with salt and pepper.

9. Whisk the eggs in a bowl, place breadcrumbs in the shallow plate and do the same with remaining butter.
10. Form the croquettes from the prepared mixture and roll them in the flour, eggs and in breadcrumbs. Repeat the process until you have no mixture left.

Freezing process:

1. Place the prepared croquettes in the food container and freeze until ready to use.

Cooking method:

1. Place the container with frozen croquettes in a bowl with hot water, for 5 minutes, just to separate them easily, if they stick to each other.
2. Heat vegetable oil in the deeper frying pan and cook croquettes for 1 ½ minute per side or until nicely golden.
3. Set on paper towel to drain and optionally serve with some lemon wedges.

Chicken Casserole

Serves: 6

Preparation time: 10 min.

Cooking time: 50 min.

Ingredients:

- 3 ½ lb. chicken breasts, cut into large pieces
- 3 tablespoons olive oil
- 2 lb. chunky vegetables – broccoli, cauliflower, bell peppers, cherry tomatoes
- 1 ½ cups chicken stock
- 1 ½ tablespoon dried thyme
- 3 tablespoons flat-leaf parsley, chopped
- 3 ¾ cups condensed cream of chicken soup
- Fresh ground salt and pepper – to taste

Preparation method:

1. Heat olive oil in non-stick pan, over medium heat and fry the chicken until slightly brown on the edges.
2. Add the thyme, stock and cream soup and mix.
3. Stir in vegetables and bring to boil. Season with salt and pepper; set aside to cool.

Freezing method:

1. You can freeze the chicken in casseroled dish or in the zip-lock bag.
2. Place in the freezer, flat position and keep until ready to use.

Cooking method:

5. Place the casserole mixture into refrigerator overnight, to thaw.

Place the prepared chicken in the casserole dish and bake for 45 minutes. Garnish with the chopped parsley before serving.

Seafood Freezer Meals

Pink Salmon Cakes

Serving: 6

Preparation time: 25 min.

Cooking time: 22 min.

Ingredients:

- 1 ½ pounds pink salmon fillets, skinless
- 1 teaspoon chili flakes
- ½ cup breadcrumbs
- 3 tablespoons mayonnaise
- 2 tablespoons Dijon mustard
- Freshly ground salt and pepper
- 2 eggs, whisked
- Lemon juice from ½ lemon
- 2 tablespoons fresh parsley, chopped
- 1 tablespoon horseradish

Preparation method:

1. Place salmon fillets onto baking tray lined with parchment paper.
2. Bake in preheated oven at 200C/400F for 15 minutes.
3. Set aside to cool and flake using fork.
4. In a large bowl combine breadcrumbs and parsley.
5. Add rest of ingredients and flaked salmon. Season with salt and pepper and stir gently until combined.
6. Form patties and wrap each in plastic foil.

Freezing method:

1. Set patties in zip-lock bags and keep in freezer for a month or until ready to use.

Cooking method:

1. Defrost patties in refrigerator overnight.
2. Heat broiler and broil patties for 6-8 minutes or until golden on top.
3. Serve with some sour cream.

Clam Chowder

Serving: 6

Preparation time: 15 min.

Cooking time: 25 min.

Reheating time: 17 min.

Ingredients:

- 24 oz. fresh or can clams, juice reserved
- 3 slices bacon, chopped
- 1 onion, diced
- 2 cups water
- 3 medium potatoes, cut in ½-inch cubes
- 2 tablespoons butter
- 1 tablespoon all-purpose flour
- Freshly ground salt and pepper
- 2 teaspoons dried basil
- 1 ½ cups cooking cream
- ½ cup milk

Preparation method:

1. In a large sauce pan cook bacon until crispy, for 5 minutes, over medium-high heat.
2. Reduce heat to low and add 1 tablespoon butter. When melted add diced onion and cook for 5 minutes.
3. Add flour and cook for 2 minutes more, stirring occasionally so flour does not burn.
4. Add water, reserved clam juice, basil and potatoes. If you use fresh clams add 2 cups chicken stock.
5. Season with salt and pepper and simmer on medium heat until potatoes are tender, for 10 minutes.
6. Reduce heat to low and add cooking cream, milk, remaining butter and clams.
7. Cook until heated through for 5 minutes. Do not boil, but simmer gently.
8. Set aside to cool.

Freezing method:

1. Pour cold chowder in container and firmly seal with lid.

2. Keep in freezer until ready to use.

Reheating method:

1. Place container in bowl with hot water for 10 minutes, so chowder can be broken in parts.
2. Place in heavy bottom sauce pan, stirring until the chowder is liquid. Add ¼ cup clam juice or milk and stir.
3. Boil for 1 minute and set aside to cool slightly before serving.

Frozen Cod

Serving: 6

Preparation time: 10 min.

Cooking time: 10 min.

Reheating time: 5 min.

Ingredients:

- 6 cod fillets, 8 oz. each
- 1 cup chopped scallions
- ½ cup minced onion
- 6 teaspoons lemon juice
- 6 garlic cloves, minced
- 3 teaspoons jalapeno peppers, chopped
- 3 tablespoons lemon zest
- 3 teaspoons olive oil
- ½ cup chopped parsley
- 1 spring rosemary, chopped
- Freshly ground salt and pepper

Preparation method:

1. Preheat oven to 200C/400F and line baking tray with aluminum foil.
2. In a medium size bowl combine parsley, rosemary, scallions, lemon juice, lemon zest, garlic, peppers and oil. Stir well.
3. Arrange cod on aluminum foil and top with prepared mixture.
4. Fold the sides of foil to form sealed packet.
5. Bake for 10 minutes and remove from the oven.
6. Leave on wire rack to cool completely.

Freezing method:

1. Place the cob in freezer plastic container and keep until ready to use.

Reheating method:

1. Thaw overnight in refrigerator and place in microwave on high for 5 minutes.
2. Serve immediately.

Frozen Stuffed Clams

Serving: 6

Preparation time: 5 min.

Cooking time: 27 min.

Ingredients:

- 14 oz. minced clams
- 12 clam shells
- 3 garlic cloves, minced
- Freshly ground salt and pepper
- 1 tablespoon onion, diced
- 2 tablespoons extra virgin olive oil
- ¼ cup breadcrumbs
- 6 slices raw bacon, cut in half
- 1 teaspoon hot sauce, like Tabasco
- 2 tablespoon fresh parsley, chopped
- 2 tablespoons water or chicken stock

Preparation method:

1. Heat olive oil in medium skillet.
2. Add onion and parsley in the skillet; cook for 2 minutes.
3. Remove from the heat and stir in hot sauce, breadcrumbs, clams, garlic and some chicken stock or water so the mixture is moist bit still holds together. Season with salt and pepper and stir well.
4. Place the clam shells in plastic container, filled with sea salt (so they stand still) spoon the mixture into shells.

Freezing method:

1. Freeze stuffed clam shells and keep until ready to use.

Cooking method:

1. Thaw clams overnight in refrigerator.
2. Preheat oven to 180C/350F and place clams on the baking sheet.

3. Top each with ½ bacon slice and bake for 25 minutes.
4. Serve while still warm with lemon wedges.

Frozen Tilapia with Bell Peppers

Serving: 6

Preparation time: 7 min.

Cooking time: 7 min.

Ingredients:

- 6 tilapia fillets
- 3 red bell peppers, sliced into strips
- 3 green bell peppers, sliced into strips
- 3 tablespoons grated Parmesan
- 3 tablespoons chopped cilantro
- 3 teaspoons crushed red pepper
- 2 cups Italian dressing
- 2 teaspoons dried basil

Preparation method:

1. Combine the Italian dressing, cilantro, red pepper and basil in a large bowl.
2. Place the sliced bell peppers and fish fillets in zip-lock bag and pour in prepared Italian dressing mixture.
3. Shake all well so fish and bell peppers are coated.

Freezing method:

1. Place the zip-lock bag in the freezer and keep until ready to use.

Cooking method:

1. Set prepared fish in the refrigerator overnight to thaw.
2. Preheat grill on medium and coat with some olive oil.
3. Toss the pepper and fish fillets on preheated grill and cook for 4 minutes on one side.
4. Transfer to the other and cook for 3 minutes more.

5. Serve immediately and sprinkle with grated Parmesan cheese.

Crab Soup

Serving: 6

Preparation time: 10 min.

Cooking time: 18 min.

Reheating time: 15 min.

Ingredients:

- 12 oz. can crab meat, drained and flaked with fork
- 1 ¼ cups half and half (or 1 cup cooking cream and ¼ cup milk)
- 1 teaspoon garlic powders
- 1 celery stalk, chopped
- 1 onion, chopped
- 10 oz. cream corn
- 8 oz. condensed cream of potato soup
- Freshly ground salt and pepper
- ½ teaspoon hot sauce, like Tabasco
- 2 tablespoons butter

- 1 cup milk
- 1 bay leaf

Preparation method:

1. In a large sauce pan melt butter and add celery and onion. Cook for 5 minutes.
2. Add rest of ingredients and stir in crab meat.
3. Cook for 13 minutes, stirring occasionally and discard bay leaf.
4. Set aside to cool completely.

Freezing method:

1. Transfer the soup to the freezer container and keep up to two months or until ready to use.

Reheating method:

1. Place the container in the large bowl filled with hot water for 3 minutes.
2. Transfer to the sauce pan and heat over medium-high heat, for 12 minutes. Add ¼ cup milk or chicken stock and stir well until heated through.

Freezer Shrimps with Cabbage

Serves: 6

Preparation time: 10 min.

Cooking time: 20 min.

Reheating time: 50 sec.

Ingredients:

- 4 lb. shrimps, cleaned
- 4 stick butter, soften at room temperature
- ¾ cup white wine
- ½ cup minced shallots
- 3 egg yolks
- 1/3 cup chopped flat-leaf parsley
- 1 ½ cup bread crumbs
- Fresh ground salt and pepper
- 1 ½ teaspoons red pepper flakes
- 10 garlic cloves, minced

- 2 lemons, juice and zest

Cabbage side dish:

- 3 cups shredded cabbage, green or red
- 1 tablespoon vegetable oil
- 1 jalapeno or chili pepper, thinly sliced
- Fresh ground salt

Preparation method:

1. Place softened butter in the food processor; add bread crumbs, scallions, parsley, egg yolks, salt, pepper, minced garlic, lemon juice, lemon zest, and red pepper flakes.
2. Transfer to the large bowl and add cleaned shrimps.
3. Toss to coat the shrimps well and let it for 10 minutes.
4. Meanwhile prepare the cabbage; heat vegetable oil in large pan and when hot add the cabbage.
5. Sauté for 5-7 minutes and season with salt and pepper.

6. Set aside to cool as well.

Freezing method:

1. Place the coated shrimps in the food containers and top with butter mixture; set in the freezer; keep until ready to use.
2. Place the cabbage in freezer bags and keep in the freezer up to 1 week.

Cooking method:

1. Place the shrimps in the refrigerator overnight to thaw. Do the same with cabbage.
2. Preheat the oven to 200C/400F and place the shrimps with butter in oven safe baking trays. You will need two. Pour over the white wine and place in the oven.
3. Bake the shrimps for 15-20 minutes and set on wire rack to cool for 5 minutes.
4. Reheat the cabbage in microwave for 40-50 seconds on high.

5. Pour the melted butter sauce over the shrimps and cabbage before serving.

Horseradish Tilapia Cakes

Serves: 6 (6x2)

Preparation time: 25 min.

Cooking time: 8 min.

Ingredients:

- 2 lb. tilapia fillets
- 2 ½ tablespoons olive oil
- 2 eggs
- ½ cup mayonnaise
- 3 tablespoons horseradish
- Juice from 2 lemons
- ½ cup chopped parsley
- 36 saltine crackers, ground to get 1 ½ cup
- Fresh ground salt and pepper

Preparation method:

1. Preheat oven to 200C/400F and brush two baking sheets with olive oil.
2. Place tilapia fillets onto baking tray and season with salt and pepper.
3. Bake for 15 minutes and set on wire rack to cool completely.
4. When cooled, use a fork to flake the fish.
5. In a large bowl combine mayonnaise, eggs, parsley lemon juice and horseradish.
6. Stir in the flaked fish and ½ saltine crackers.
7. Season with salt and pepper and stir well to combine.
8. Form 12 cakes and gently roll them in the remaining crumbled crackers.

Freezing method:

1. Place the tilapia cakes in the food container, lined with parchment paper and set in the freezer. Keep until ready to use.

Cooking method:

1. Place the container with the cakes in a bowl filled with hot water for 5 minutes.
2. Heat some oil in non-stick pan over medium-high heat and cook the cakes for 6-8 minutes per side.
3. Set on paper towel and sprinkle with lemon juice before serving.

Simple Salmon Loaf

Serves: 6

Preparation time: 10 min.

Cooking time: 30 min.

Ingredients:

- 4 lb. can salmon, flaked
- ½ cup chopped fresh parsley
- 4 tablespoons butter, melted
- 2 cups potato chips, crushed
- 4 eggs, whisked
- 1 teaspoon red pepper flakes

Preparation method:

1. Combine all ingredients in a large bowl.
2. Divide into two loaf pans and wrap with parchment paper.

Freezing method:

1. Place the salmon loaf in the freezer and keep until ready to use.

Cooking method:

1. Set the salmon loaf in the refrigerator overnight to thaw.
2. Preheat oven to 200C/400F and place the salmon loafs onto baking tray lined with parchment paper.
3. Drizzle with olive oil and bake for 30 minutes.
4. Remove from the oven and cool slightly before serving.

Orange Salmon with Veggies

Serves: 6

Preparation time: 10 min.

Cooking time: 10 min.

Ingredients:

- 2 ½ lb. salmon fillets
- 2 tablespoons tablespoon teriyaki sauce
- ½ cup maple syrup
- 1 cup fresh squeezed orange juice
- 2 teaspoons orange zest
- ½ teaspoon lime zest
- 3 cups asparagus, cut into 2-inch pieces
- 2 cups onion, chopped

Preparation method:

1. In a small bowl combine orange zest, lime zest, orange juice, teriyaki sauce and maple syrup.
2. Place salmon fillets and veggies in a zip-lock bag and pour in prepared mixture.
3. Shake well until salmon and veggies are coated.

Freezing method:

1. Place the salmon in the flat position and freeze; keep until ready to use.

Cooking method:

1. Set the salmon and veggies in the refrigerator overnight to thaw.
2. Preheat grill pan and bake salmon, skin side down, for 10-12 minutes or just until salmon starts to flakes. Remove the salmon from the pan and add some oil. Cook vegetables for 2 minutes, stirring constantly.
3. Serve over salmon while still warm.

Creole Shrimps with Couscous

Serves: 6

Preparation time: 10 min.

Cooking time: 11 min.

Reheating time: 25 min.

Ingredients:

- 2 lb. cooked shrimps
- 3 tablespoons vegetable oil
- 1 onion, chopped
- 1 red bell pepper, chopped
- 3 garlic cloves, minced
- 14 oz. can diced tomatoes
- 8 oz. tomato sauce
- 1 tablespoon hot sauce
- 2 teaspoons sugar
- 2 teaspoons celery salt

- ¼ teaspoon cayenne pepper
- 2 tablespoon chopped parsley

For the couscous:
- 2 cups vegetable stock
- 1 ½ cups couscous
- Large pinch of salt

Preparation method:

1. Heat vegetable oil in the medium size pan and when it starts to simmer, add onion and bell pepper. Sauté for 10 minutes or until tender, over medium heat.
2. Add garlic and cook for 1 minute or until it becomes very fragrant.
3. Add remaining ingredients, stir well to combine and remove from the heat.
4. Set aside to cool.
5. Meanwhile prepare the couscous; bring the vegetable stock to boil over medium-high heat.
6. Stir in the couscous; remove from the heat and let it stand for 5 minutes.
7. Flake with the fork and set aside to cool.

Freezing method:

1. Pour the mixture, with shrimps into zip-lock freezer bags and set in freezer, in a flat position. Keep until ready to use and do the same with the couscous.

Reheating method:

1. Place the zip-lock bag in the refrigerator overnight to thaw.
2. Place the shrimps, with sauce in medium sauce pan and heat until it starts to simmer.
3. Simmer for 20 minutes and serve while still hot.
4. Reheating couscous; let it thaw overnight in refrigerator. Place couscous in the pan and add ¼ cup of vegetable stock. Reheat for 5 minutes over medium-high heat. Serve with shrimps.

Spicy Red Snapper with Cooked Rice

Serves: 6

Preparation time: 10 min.

Cooking time: 10 min.

Ingredients:

- 6 red snapper fillets, medium size
- 3 tablespoons teriyaki sauce
- 1 teaspoon red pepper flakes
- ¼ teaspoon chili powder
- 6 tablespoons lemon juice
- 6 tablespoons olive oil
- 2 cups cooked rice
- ½ cup grated parmesan

Preparation method:

1. Place the teriyaki sauce, lemon juice, spices and oil in food processor.
2. Pulse until well combined.

Freezing method:

1. Place the red snapper fillets in zip-lock freezer bags and pour in prepared mixture.
2. Seal the bag and shake well, so fish fillets are coated.
3. Place in the freezer; flat position.

Cooking method:

1. Set the salmon fillets into refrigerator overnight to thaw.
2. Place the red snapper fillets on broiler pan, skin side down.
3. Broil for 8-10 minutes, 6-inches from heat or until fish starts to flake.
5. Serve while still hot with cooked rice and sprinkle over grated parmesan.

Seafood Chowder

Serves: 6

Preparation time: 10 min.

Cooking time: 15 min.

Reheating time: 25 min.

Ingredients:

- 3 medium potatoes, peeled and diced
- 1 carrot, finely chopped
- 1 celery stalk, finely chopped
- 4 cups chicken or fish stock
- 1 ½ cup corn kernels
- 1 ¼ lb. marinara seafood mix
- 1 cup thickened cream
- 2 tablespoons chopped chives
- 2 tablespoons chopped parsley
- Fresh ground salt and pepper –to taste

Preparation method:

1. Place potatoes, carrot, stock and celery in a large pan.
2. Cover and bring to boil; reduce heat and simmer for 10 minutes.
3. Remove from the heat and using hand blender, mix until smooth.
4. Add corn kernels to the soup and simmer again for 10 minutes.
5. Reduce the heat and add seafood mix and cream.
6. Stir and cook, without boiling for 5 minutes or until seafood is cooked.
7. Season to taste and add chives and parsley.
8. Set aside to cool.

Freezing method:

1. Pour the cooled chowder in airtight container and place in the freezer; keep until ready to use.

Reheating method:

1. Place the airtight container in the bowl filled with hot water.
2. Transfer the chowder to the pot and heat over medium heat.
3. Stir the stew, gently to distribute heat evenly, but do not press because you may break the seafood and end up with the mush.
4. Bring stew to boil (you will need 25 minutes) and remove from the heat.
5. Serve immediately.

Pork Freezer Meals

Pork and Plums

Serving: 6

Preparation time: 7 min.

Cooking time: 30 min.

Reheating time: 12 min.

Ingredients:

- 2 lb. cooked pork, cut into strips
- 1 cup chopped dried plums
- 1 cup beef stock
- 1 tablespoon cornstarch
- ½ cup brown sugar
- 1 tablespoon lime juice
- 2 tablespoon butter
- 1 bay leaf

Preparation method:

1. In a sauce pan combine brown sugar, beef broth and cornstarch. Stir well until smooth and without lumps.
2. Add bay leaf and cook for 5-7 minutes on low.
3. Add plums, lime juice and butter. Cook on high until boils.
4. Preheat oven to 180C/350F and place pork in casserole dish. Pour over prepared mixture and place in preheated oven. Bake for 20 minutes.
5. Set aside until cooled completely.

Freezing method:

1. Transfer pork to freezer containers and place in freezer. Keep until ready to use.

Reheating method:

1. Place containers under hot water for 5 minutes or overnight in refrigerator until thawed.
2. Place the pork meat in large sauce pan and reheat until heated through for 7 minutes.
3. Serve immediately.

Almond Meal Breaded Pork Chops

Serving: 6

Preparation time: 12 min.

Cooking time: 20 min.

Ingredients:

- 6 bone-in pork chops, around 1-inch thick
- 2 cups almond meal
- Freshly ground salt and pepper
- 3 eggs, whisked
- ¼ cup butter, melted
- ¼ cup sunflower oil
- 1 tablespoon fresh thyme, chopped
- 2 teaspoons ground cumin

Preparation method:

1. Whisk eggs and thyme in a large bowl. Set aside.

2. Place pork chops between two pieces plastic foil and beat with heavy-bottom sauce pan, to ¼-inch thick. Try to avoid the bone.
3. Pace almond meal in shallow dish and season with salt and pepper.
4. Season pork chops with salt and pepper and dip in the eggs.
5. Gently shake to remove excess and place in almond meal, to coat well.

Freezing method:

1. Wrap each pork chop in freezer paper and set in zip-lock bags.
2. Freeze and keep up to 5 weeks.

Cooking method:

1. Place pork chops in the refrigerator overnight to thaw.
2. Preheat grill pan and combine butter and oil in small bowl.
3. Brush pork chops, both sides, with oil mixture and cook until deep gold, both sides for 10 minutes.

4. Serve while still warm.

Apple Pork Chops

Serving: 6

Preparation time: 5 min.

Cooking time: 27 min.

Ingredients:

- 6 pork chops, boneless
- 1 ½ cups beef stock
- ½ cup apple cider
- ½ cup apple puree
- 4 teaspoons balsamic vinegar
- Freshly ground pepper
- 3 tablespoons olive oil
- 3 tablespoons cornstarch

Preparation method:

1. Season pork chops with pepper.

2. Place in freezer zip-lock bag and add rest of ingredients, except olive oil.
3. Shake well and set in the freezer.

Freezing method:

1. Place the zip-lock bag flat and keep for 5 weeks or until ready to use.

Cooking method:

1. Set pork chops in refrigerate overnight to thaw.
2. Heat olive oil in large skillet and add only pork chops, not the sauce.
3. Cook pork chops until browned, for 5 minutes, remove from the pan and add the sauce.
4. Pour the sauce and cook for 20 minutes.
5. Add 3 tablespoons of cornstarch and bring to boil over medium-high heat, whisking until thick.
6. Add the chops back in the pan and set simmer for 1 minute.
7. Serve pork chops immediately with sauce on top.

Pork Meatballs

Serving: 6

Preparation time: 15 min.

Cooking time: 20 min.

Ingredients:

- 2 lb. ground pork
- 2 eggs, whisked
- 1 cup grated Parmesan
- 1 tablespoon olive oil
- ½ cup bread crumbs
- 4 garlic cloves, minced
- 1 teaspoon ground cumin
- 1 teaspoon chili flakes
- Freshly ground salt and pepper
- 1/3 cup chopped parsley
- 2 cups tomato sauce

Preparation method:

1. In a large bowl combine pork meat, garlic, chili flakes, breadcrumbs, olive oil, eggs, Parmesan cheese, cumin and parsley. Season with salt and pepper and mix with hands.
2. Form meatballs from the mixture and arrange onto baking tray lined with parchment paper.

Freezing method:

1. Place meatballs in freezer, on baking sheet, and freeze for couple hours. Transfer to the zip-lock bag and keep in freezer until ready to use.

Cooking method:

1. Set meatballs in refrigerator overnight until thawed.
2. Heat some olive oil and cook meatballs until browned on all sides, for 7 minutes, over medium high heat.
3. Add tomato sauce and cook for 13 minutes. Season with salt and pepper and serve.

Green Peppers Stuffed with Pork

Serving: 6

Preparation time: 15 min.

Cooking time: 30 min.

Ingredients:

- 6 green bell peppers
- 1 ¼ lb. ground pork, cooked and drained
- 1 onion, finely chopped
- 3 garlic cloves, minced
- 8 oz. tomato sauce
- 1 cup rice, cooked
- 3 tablespoons shredded cheese – by your choice
- Freshly ground salt and pepper

Preparation method:

1. Cut the tops of the peppers and remove the seeds. Cut off the bottom, so they can stand.
2. In a bowl combine browned pork meat, garlic, cooked rice, tomato sauce and season with salt and pepper.
3. Stir well to combine and stuff bell peppers almost to the top.

Freezing method:

1. Arrange bell peppers on baking sheet and set to freezer for couple hours.
2. Transfer to the zip-lock bag and keep until ready to use.

Cooking method:

1. Place bell peppers in refrigerator overnight to thaw.
2. Preheat oven to 180C/350F and line baking tray with parchment paper.
3. Set bell peppers on baking tray, sprinkle with cheese and place in the oven; bake for 30 minutes.

4. Serve while still warm.

Pork Casserole

Serves: 6

Preparation time: 10 min.

Cooking time: 57 min.

Ingredients:

- 3 cups diced ham
- 4 green onions, chopped
- 4 eggs, whisked
- 15 oz. creamed corn
- 12 oz. Mexican corn
- 8 oz. corn muffin mix
- 2 cups shredded cheddar cheese
- 1 ½ sticks butter, melted

Preparation method:

1. Combine all ingredients, except cheese in a large bowl.

2. Pour into foil pan, cover with plastic foil and with aluminum foil.
3. Place the shredded cheese in another zip-lock bag and set in the freezer.

Freezing method:

1. Set in the freezer, flat position and keep until ready to use.

Cooking method:

1. Place the casserole ingredients in a refrigerator or overnight to thaw.
2. Grease oven proof baking dish (7x11) and transfer the casserole ingredients in the dish.
3. Bake in preheated oven at 180C/356F for 55 minutes.
4. Sprinkle with cheese and bake for 2 minutes more.
5. Serve while still hot

Pork Tenderloin with Beer

Serves: 6

Preparation time: 10 min.

Cooking time: 18 min.

Ingredients:

- 2 pork tenderloins, about 12 oz. each
- ½ cup non-alcoholic beer
- 1/3 cup lemon juice
- 3 garlic cloves, minced
- 2 tablespoons chopped fresh parsley
- ½ teaspoon ground cumin
- ¼ teaspoon chili flakes
- ½ teaspoon chili powder
- Fresh ground salt and pepper

Preparation method:

1. In a large bowl whisk lemon juice, beer, spices, parsley, cumin and garlic.
2. Add pork and turn couple times to coat.

Freezing method:

1. Place the pork tenderloin in two zip-lock freezer bags.
2. Set in the freezer and keep up to a month or until ready to use.

Cooking method:

1. Place the tenderloin in refrigerator overnight to thaw.
2. Place pork on preheated grill over medium high heat and brush with some marinade.
3. Close with the lid and cook, flipping occasionally for 18 minutes.
4. Transfer to the cutting board and cover with aluminum foil; let it rest for 5 minutes before slicing.

Mustard Pork Chops with Applesauce

Serves: 6

Preparation time: 15 min.

Cooking time: 25 min.

Ingredients:

- 6 pork chops, boneless
- ½ cup honey
- 2 teaspoons Dijon mustard
- Fresh ground salt and pepper

For the apple sauce:

- 2 ½ cups apple sauce
- ¼ cup brown sugar
- ¼ teaspoon cinnamon
- 1 teaspoon ground mustard
- 1 small onion, thinly sliced

- Fresh ground salt and pepper

Preparation method:

1. Combine mustard and honey in a bowl and add salt and pepper.
2. Stir well to combine.
3. Place the pork chops in the freezer dish and top with mustard mixture.
4. Cover tightly with aluminum foil and place in the freezer.
5. Combine the apple sauce, onion, cinnamon, ground mustard and salt and pepper in a bowl.

Freezing method:

1. Place the freezer dish with pork chops in the freezer and keep up to 1 month or until ready to use. Place the apple sauce in another zip-lock bag.

Cooking method:

1. Place the pork chops and apple sauce in refrigerator overnight to thaw.
2. Preheat oven to 220C/425F.
3. Arrange pork chops onto rimmed baking tray and pour over thawed apple sauce; bake pork chops for 25 minutes.
4. Serve while still hot.

Spicy Pork Soup

Serves: 6

Preparation time: 5 min.

Cooking time: 25 min.

Reheating time: 22 min.

Ingredients:

- 1 lb. ground pork
- 3 garlic cloves, minced
- 3 teaspoons finely grated ginger
- ½ teaspoon crushed red pepper flakes
- 6 cups chicken stock
- 4 scallions, finely sliced
- 3 tablespoons soy sauce
- 10 oz. rice noodles
- 2 tablespoons vegetable oil
- 5 cups mustard greens
- Fresh ground salt and pepper
- 1 teaspoon cumin seeds

Preparation method:

1. Combine pork, cumin, red pepper flakes and ginger in a large bowl.
2. Heat oil in large pot over medium high heat.
3. Add pork mixture and season with salt and pepper.
4. Cook for 8-10 minutes or until browned.
5. Add stock and bring to boil; reduce heat to medium and simmer for 8-10 minutes.
6. Add scallions, soy sauce and cook for 5 minutes.
7. Season additionally with salt and pepper.

Freezing method:

1. Pour the cooled soup in zip-lock bags and place in the freezer, flat position.
2. Keep in the freezer until ready to use.

Reheating method:

1. Place the zip-lock bag with the soup in a bowl filled with hot water.
2. Let it sit for 5-7 minutes and transfer to the pot.
3. Heat over medium heat, stirring occasionally to distribute the heat.
4. Cook for 15 minutes and stir in torn mustard greens and rice noodles.
5. Cook additionally for 5-7 minutes and serve while still hot.

Pork Pies

Serves: 6

Preparation time: 15 min.

Cooking time: 35 min.

Ingredients:

- 1 ¼ lb. pork sausages
- 1 apple, grated
- 2 ¼ cups plain flour
- 1 egg, whisked
- 1 egg yolk, whisked
- 2 tablespoons butter
- 1 tablespoon chopped parsley
- ¼ teaspoon ground nutmeg
- Fresh ground salt and pepper
- ½ cup water

Preparation method:

1. Squeeze sausage meat from the casings into a bowl.
2. Add grated apple, nutmeg, parsley and season with salt and pepper.
3. Mix well to combine and set aside.
4. In separate bowl combine flour, pinch of salt with water and melted butter.
5. Add whisked egg and continue mixing with hands until you have a smooth ball.
6. Roll the dough onto floured surface and using cookie cutter, cut out 6 rounds from the dough.
7. Place the rounds into greased muffin tin, leaving slight overhang.
8. Divide the sausage meat between muffin holes.
9. Knead the remaining pastry and roll out once again; cut 6 more rounds and top the sausage meat.
10. Wrap with aluminum foil and freeze.

Freezing method:

1. Place the muffin tin in the freezer and keep until ready to use.

Cooking method:

1. Place the pork pies in refrigerator overnight to thaw.
2. Preheat oven to 200C/400F and brush pies with the whisked egg yolk. Sprinkle it with some coarse sea salt.
3. Bake the pies for 35 minutes or until golden.
4. Set on wire rack to cool slightly before serving.

Pork Empanadas

Serves: 6

Preparation time: 20 min.

Cooking time: 30 min.

Ingredients:

- 1 lb. ground pork
- 2 tablespoons olive oil
- 2 teaspoons fresh sage
- 1 onion, diced
- 4 teaspoons flour
- 4 tablespoons water
- Fresh ground salt and pepper
- 2 garlic cloves, minced

For the pastry:

- 3 cups flour
- 2 teaspoons baking powder

- 1 ½ sticks butter, diced
- 1 egg
- 1 ¼ cup water, cold
- ½ teaspoon salt

Preparation method: Dough

1. Place sage, flour, baking powder and salt in food processor.
2. Pulse a couple of times and add butter; pulse a couple of times until you have mixture similar to coarse meal.
3. Add water and pulse again, until a ball forms. Transfer the dough to the floured kitchen surface and knead until it comes together.
4. Divide the dough in half and roll out on floured kitchen surface, until 1/8-inch thick.
5. Using a cookie cutter, 7-inch wide, cut out rounds. Knead the remaining dough, roll it out and continue cutting until you have 6 rounds.

Preparation method: The filling

1. Heat some oil in a large skillet and when hot add onion.
2. Cook for 10 minutes over medium-high heat and add garlic, pork and sage.
3. Mix in the flour and cook for 30 seconds.
4. Add 4 tablespoons of water and stir until thick.
5. Remove from the heat and season with salt and pepper.
6. Place 1/6 of the filling onto pastry, leaving a ½-inch border around the edge.
7. Brush the edges with water and fold the pastry over the filling. Pinch edges with fork.

Freezing method:

1. Place the empanadas on baking sheet and place into freezer, until firm.
2. Transfer to the airtight container and keep in the freezer until ready to use.

Cooking method:

1. Preheat oven to 200C/400F and line baking tray with parchment paper.
2. Brush empanadas with some vegetable oil or whisked egg yolk and arrange ½-inch apart on baking sheet.
3. Bake for 30 minutes or until golden.

Vegetarian Freezer Meals

Black Bean Burgers

Serving: 6

Preparation time: 15 min.

Cooking time: 12 min.

Ingredients:

- 28 oz. black beans, drained and rinsed
- 1 cup brown rice, cooked
- 2 onions, finely chopped
- ½ teaspoon ground cumin
- 1 teaspoon chili flakes
- 1 tablespoon olive oil
- 1 tablespoon lime juice
- Freshly ground salt and pepper
- 1 tablespoon chopped parsley

Preparation method:

1. Place half of beans and onions in food processor.

2. Add cumin and chili flakes; pulse until you have thick paste.
3. Transfer to the large bowl and remaining beans, lime juice, rice, parsley and season with salt and pepper. Stir well to combine.
4. Form 6 patties from the mixture and wrap each in wax paper.

Freezing method:

1. Place wrapped patties in the zip-lock bag and keep until ready to use.

Cooking method:

1. Place frozen burgers in the refrigerator overnight, to thaw.
2. Preheat oven to 200C/400F and line baking sheet with parchment paper.
3. Arrange patties on the baking sheet and bake for 12 minutes, until nicely gold.
4. Serve while still hot with some thick yogurt.

Vegetarian Chili

Serving: 6

Preparation time: 5 min.

Cooking time: 30 min.

Reheating timc: 12 min.

Ingredients:

- 1 ½ cups can black beans, rinsed
- 1 ½ cups can kidney beans, rinsed
- 1 tablespoon chili powder
- 1/8 teaspoon cayenne pepper
- 1 teaspoon ground cumin
- 1 small zucchini, diced
- 20 oz. can crushed tomatoes
- 1 jalapeno pepper, diced
- 1 cup can corn
- 1 red bell pepper, diced
- 2 tablespoons tomato paste
- 1 onion, diced

- 2 garlic cloves minced

Preparation method:

1. Heat some oil in Dutch oven over medium-high heat.
2. Add onion and cook for 5 minutes.
3. Add garlic, cumin, chili powder and cayenne pepper; cook for 1 minute.
4. Stir in the zucchini and red bell pepper; cook for 7 minutes.
5. Add beans, crushed tomatoes with juice, tomato paste and corn.
6. Stir well and bring to boil over medium heat.
7. Reduce heat to low and simmer for 20 minutes.
8. Season with salt and pepper and remove from the heat.
9. When cooled transfer to the container or zip-lock freezer bags.

Freezing method:

1. Pack the chili in 6 freezer bags, because heating larger amount will take too much of your time.

2. Keep in the freezer, flat position, until ready to use.

Reheating method:

1. Set in microwave on high for 2 minutes.
2. Transfer to the sauce pan and heat over medium high heat for 10 minutes.
3. Serve while still hot.

Vegetarian Calzones

Serving: 6

Preparation time: 15 min.

Cooking time: 35 min.

Ingredients:

- 2 lb. bought pizza dough, 6 pieces
- 3 cups cooked mixed veggies, like mushrooms, spinach and kale
- 1 cup vegetarian creamy cheese
- Freshly ground salt and pepper
- 6 tablespoons tomato puree
- Some olive oil

Preparation method:

1. Place the dough between two pieces of parchment paper and roll out with rolling pin, to 8-inch large circle.

2. In a large bowl combine veggies and creamy cheese; season with salt and pepper and stir well to combine.
3. Spread 1 tablespoon of tomato puree over pizza dough and top with 1/6 of the veggie mixture, leaving a clean border around the edge.
4. Fold the dough and over the filing and pinch to seal.

Freezing method:

1. Wrap calzones in wax paper and place in zip-lock bags.
2. Transfer to the freezer and keep until ready to use.

Cooking method:

1. Preheat oven to 180C/350F and line baking tray with parchment paper.
2. Brush calzones with olive oil and bake for 35 minutes.
3. Set aside to cool slightly before serving.

Vegetable Soup

Serving: 6

Preparation time: 15 min.

Cooking time: 12 min.

Reheating time: 8 min.

Ingredients:

- 6 cups chicken stock
- 1 small onion, diced
- 1 celery stalk, chopped
- ½ cup diced carrots
- 1 garlic clove, minced
- 15 oz. canned tomatoes
- 16 oz. kidney beans, rinsed
- 1 cup chopped endive
- ½ cup shredded vegetarian Parmesan-like cheese
- Freshly ground pepper
- 1 cup diced zucchinis

Preparation method:

1. In a medium sauce pan heat oil and cook onion, celery and carrots for 5 minutes, over medium heat.
2. Add garlic and cook for 1 minute more, stirring occasionally.
3. Add the tomatoes, chicken stock and kidney beans.
4. Bring to boil over high heat and boil for 1 minute.
5. Remove from the heat and cool.

Freezing method:

1. When cooled fully, transfer to the freezer zip-lock bags and freeze flat. Keep until ready to use.

Reheating method:

1. Set in refrigerator overnight to thaw.
2. Place in the sauce pan and bring to boil over high heat.
3. Add endive and season with pepper.

4. Simmer for 5 minutes and stir in the cheese.
5. Serve when cooled slightly.

Chickpea Pot Pie

Serving: 6

Preparation time: 15 min.

Cooking time: 30 min.

Ingredients:

- 10 oz. cream of mushroom soup
- 1 ½ cups caramelized onion
- 2 tablespoon soy milk
- 1 cup peas
- ½ cup diced carrots
- ½ cup corn
- 2 9-inch pie crusts
- 1 teaspoon dried basil
- 1 cup cooked chickpea

Preparation method:

1. Combine all ingredients, except pie crusts.

2. Grease pie pan with olive oil and place one pie crust.
3. Add prepared mixture and top with second pie crust. Make few slices on the top, to release steam while cooking.

Freezing method:

1. Wrap pie in the wax paper and set in the freezer.
2. Keep in the freezer until ready to use.

Cooking method:

1. Set frozen pie in the freezer overnight.
2. Preheat oven to 200C/400F and bake pie for 30 minutes.
3. Cool slightly before slicing.

Quinoa Cakes

Serves: 6

Preparation time: 7 min.

Cooking time: 10 min.

Reheating timc: 90 scc.

Ingredients:

- 1 ½ cups quinoa
- 2 eggs, whisked
- ½ tablespoon garlic, minced
- 2 tablespoons flour
- 1 tablespoon olive oil
- 2 tablespoons shallots, diced
- 2 tablespoons breadcrumbs
- Fresh ground salt and pepper
- 3 tablespoons shredded Parmesan cheese
- Fresh salad – to serve

Preparation method:

1. Place all ingredients in a bowl, except olive oil, and let it stand for 5 minutes.
2. Form 6 patties and cook in heated olive oil in large pan, 5 minutes per side.
3. Place on paper towels to drain.

Freezing method:

1. Wrap the cooked patties in the parchment paper and place in airtight container.
2. Freeze until ready to use.

Reheating method:

1. Place the patties in microwave and heat on medium-high for 90 seconds. Serve with some fresh salad.

Rice Herbs and Cheese Balls

Serves: 6

Preparation time: 10 min.

Cooking time: 10 min.

Reheating time: 20 min.

Ingredients:

- 2 cups cooked rice, warm
- 2 eggs
- 1 ½ cups breadcrumbs
- 3 tablespoons grated parmesan cheese
- 1 tablespoon chopped parsley
- 1 teaspoon dried thyme
- 1 teaspoon dried sage
- 2 teaspoons dried basil
- Fresh ground salt and pepper – to taste
- 28 oz. tomato sauce

Preparation method:

1. Whisk the eggs, fresh ground salt, pepper, parsley and cheese.
2. Stir the egg mixture into warm rice and set aside to cool. Stir in the remaining herbs.
3. Form balls from the prepared mixture and coat them into breadcrumbs.
4. Heat oil in a nonstick skillet over medium heat. Cook the meatballs in the oil for 8-10 minutes, turning carefully, until light golden brown.
5. Drain meatballs on paper towels. Gently mix meatballs with tomato sauce.

Freezing method:

1. Place the rice balls, with sauce in zip-lock bag and freeze in flat position.

Reheating method:

1. Set the rice balls in refrigerator overnight, to thaw.

2. Place the rice balls in a saucepan and heat over medium low heat, stirring occasionally, until meatballs are hot all the way through, for 20 min.
3. Serve with some spaghetti.

Eggplant Lasagna

Serves: 6

Preparation time: 30 min.

Cooking time: 1 h. 10 min.

Ingredients:

- 1 ½ cup breadcrumbs
- 2 eggs, whisked with 1 tablespoon water
- 0.8 oz. grated Parmesan cheese
- 2 eggplants, medium size, cut into ½-inch rounds
- Fresh ground salt and pepper

Filling:

- ¼ cup grated Parmesan cheese
- 12 oz. ricotta cheese
- 1 egg, whisked
- 20 oz. tomato sauce
- Fresh ground salt and pepper

- 3 garlic cloves, minced
- 7 oz. mozzarella cheese

Preparation method:

1. Combine bread crumbs and parmesan cheese in a shallow dish.
2. Dip the eggplant slices in the egg mixture, drain the excess and dip in the breadcrumbs to coat well.
3. Place onto lined baking tray and bake in preheated oven at 180C/356F for 30 minutes.
4. Set aside to cool; meanwhile prepare the filling.
5. Combine all the egg, fresh ground salt and pepper, minced garlic, ricotta and parmesan cheese.
6. Assembling; place some of the tomato sauce in the bottom of baking dish.
7. Layer half of the eggplant slices over tomato sauce and top with ¾ cup sauce. Spread half of the filling mixture and top with 1/3 of mozzarella slices.

8. Repeat the process ending with tomato sauce.

Freezing method:

1. Cover the baking dish with the aluminum foil and tightly wrap with plastic foil.
2. Set in the freezer and keep until ready to use.

Cooking method:

1. Place the eggplant lasagna in refrigerator overnight to thaw.
2. Preheat the oven to 180C/356F and bake the lasagna for 35-40 minutes.
3. Set on wire rack to cool before slicing.

NOTE: You can bake lasagna from frozen condition, but prolong baking for 10 minutes more.

Stuffed Peppers

Serves: 6

Preparation time: 15 min.

Cooking time: 36 min.

Ingredients:

- 6 red or green bell peppers
- 1 cup cooked rice
- 1 ½ cup cooked red lentils
- 1 cup yellow onion, chopped
- 2 cups chopped spinach
- 1 tablespoon vegetable oil
- 3 garlic cloves, minced
- 1 teaspoon ground cumin
- 1 teaspoon tomato puree
- Fresh ground salt and pepper

Preparation method:

1. Heat oil in medium pan and when hot add onion; cook for 5 minutes; add garlic, cumin, tomato puree and cook further for 1 minute.
2. Add the lentils, rice and season with salt and pepper.
3. Stir in the chopped spinach; cook for 1 minute and remove from the heat.
4. Cut the tops from the pepper and remove the seeds.
5. Carefully cut the bottom of the peppers, so they can stand upright.
6. Fill each bell pepper with prepared mixture.

Freezing method:

1. Wrap the bell peppers in parchment paper and place in the freezer bags.
2. Set in the freezer and keep until ready to use.

Cooking method:

1. Set the peppers in refrigerator overnight to thaw.

2. Preheat the oven to 200C/400F and grease baking dish with some oil.
3. Place the peppers, upright, in the baking dish and bake for 30 minutes.
4. Serve with some toasted bread.

Vegetable Stew

Serves: 6

Preparation time: 30 min.

Cooking time: 3 min.

Reheating time: 20 min.

Ingredients:

- 3 zucchinis
- 2 eggplants
- 2 green peppers
- 4 tomatoes, large and ripe, peeled
- 1 tablespoon chopped basil
- Fresh ground salt and pepper
- 2 brown onions, medium
- 3 garlic cloves, minced
- 4 tablespoons vegetable oil
- 1 spring thyme – leaves only
- 1 tablespoon red wine vinegar
- 1 cup vegetable stock

Preparation method:

1. Chop eggplants and zucchinis in 2-inch slices; season with salt and pepper and set in colander for 30 minutes. Press veggies with a plate.
2. Meanwhile chop the peppers and onion; set aside.
3. To peel the tomatoes; make the "x" sign on the bottom of tomatoes. Place them in the pot with boiling water for 20 seconds and transfer them into ice cold water for 10 seconds.
4. Using a knife peel the tomatoes and remove the seeds; chop roughly.
5. Heat olive oil in large pot and add onion and garlic. Cook over medium heat for 5 minutes, stirring frequently. Add vegetable stock and bring to boil. Reduce heat to medium and cook for 2 minutes more.
6. Add drained eggplants.
7. Add basil and season with salt and pepper.
8. Cover the pot and simmer the veggies for 20 minutes.

9. Add the tomatoes and vinegar; cook for 5 minutes more. Stir in the zucchinis and cook for 5 minutes.
10. Set aside to cool.

Freezing method:

1. Place the veggies in airtight container and set in the freezer.
2. Keep until ready to use.

Reheating method:

1. Place frozen veggies in the large pot and add 2 tablespoons vegetable stock.
2. Heat over medium heat, slowly for 20 minutes.
3. Do not stir frequently because vegetables may become mushy.
4. Serve immediately.

Conclusion

I hope sincerely you enjoyed this book!

It is my deep desire that you enjoy a life full of energy and vitality!

Keep creating new recipes and having fun with the process!

Did you like this book?

If you enjoyed this book - please give your review on Amazon about it!

If you believe this book is worth sharing, would you take a few seconds to let your friends know about it? If it turns out to make a difference in their lives, they'll be forever grateful to you.

As I will.

All the best,

Morgan White

Highly Recommended

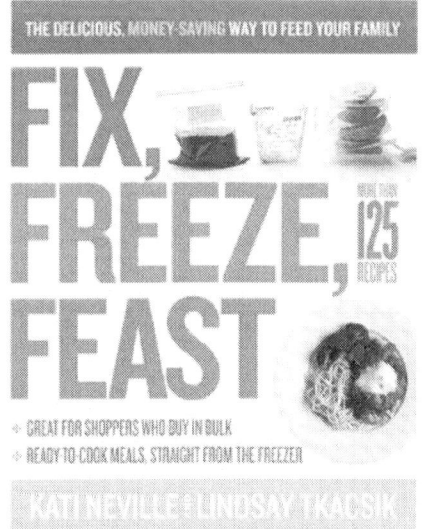

Other Books by Morgan White

Printed in Great Britain
by Amazon